GREEK MYTHOLOGY

POSEIDON,

God of the Sea

BY JOANNA BLAIR

Enslow
PUBLISHING

Please visit our website, www.enslow.com. For a free color catalog of all our high-quality books, call toll free 1-800-398-2504 or fax 1-877-980-4454.

Cataloging-in-Publication Data
Names: Blair, Joanna.
Title: Poseidon, god of the sea / Joanna Blair.
Description: Buffalo, NY : Enslow Publishing, 2027. | Series: Greek mythology | Includes glossary and index.
Identifiers: ISBN 9781978550957 (pbk.) | ISBN 9781978550964 (library bound) | ISBN 9781978550971 (ebook)
Subjects: LCSH: Poseidon (Greek deity)--Juvenile literature. | Gods, Greek--Juvenile literature. | Mythology, Greek--Juvenile literature.
Classification: LCC BL820.N5 B535 2027 | DDC 292.2113--dc23

Published in 2027 by
Enslow Publishing
2544 Clinton Street
Buffalo, NY 14224

Portions of this work were originally authored by Christine Ha and published as *Poseidon*. All new material in this edition was authored by Joanna Blair.

Cover Designer: Joshua Olson
Interior Designer: Joshua Olson
Editor: Claire Vanden Branden

Photo Credits: Cover, p. 1 Zwiebackesser/Shutterstock.com; pp. 4–5 eurobanks/Shutterstock.com; pp. 6–7 Alexandre Rotenberg/Shutterstock.com; p. 8 stockfootagekz/Shutterstock.com; pp. 9, 29 WH_Pics/Shutterstock.com; pp. 10–11 Ray T./Shutterstock.com; pp. 12–13 Malchev/Shutterstock.com; pp. 14–15 cpaulfell/Shutterstock.com; pp. 16–17 Anton Balazh/Shutterstock.com; pp. 18–19 Michael Rosskothen/Shutterstock.com; pp. 20–21 Sergey Mikhaylov/Shutterstock.com; pp. 22–23 Georgios Tsichlis/Shutterstock.com; pp. 24–25 Adam Friesen/Shutterstock.com; p. 26 neurobit/Shutterstock.com; p. 27 Nosyrevy/Shutterstock.com.

Printed in China

CPSIA compliance information: Batch #QS27ENS: For further information contact Enslow Publishing, at 1-800-398-2504.

TABLE OF CONTENTS

CHAPTER 1

OCEAN RULER

Poseidon was the Greek god of the sea. He could cause storms, floods, and earthquakes.

Poseidon was one of the 12 main Greek gods.

Amphitrite was queen of the sea.

Poseidon lived at the bottom of the sea. He had a beautiful palace there. It was made of gems and coral.

Legends say many nymphs lived in the ocean. One became Poseidon's wife. Her name was Amphitrite.

Poseidon protected sailors who traveled by sea. He guided their ships to safety. But if he got angry, he could send waves or storms.

Poseidon had many children. Some were monsters or sea creatures.

Legends say Poseidon was the father of the winged horse, Pegasus.

Triton was one of Poseidon's sons. He had the tail of a fish.

LORD OF HORSES

Poseidon was also the god of horses. Stories said he created the first horse. He struck his **trident** against a rock. A horse jumped out.

CHAPTER 2

FAMOUS MYTHS

Poseidon, Hades, and Zeus were brothers. In one myth, they freed some giants. As a reward, the giants gave Poseidon a trident with magic powers.

Poseidon used his trident to control the sea.

Poseidon's one-eyed son owned sheep.

One of Poseidon's sons was a one-eyed giant. In one myth, a hero blinded this son. To get revenge, Poseidon sent a storm to stop the hero's ships.

The hero who fought Poseidon's son was named Odysseus.

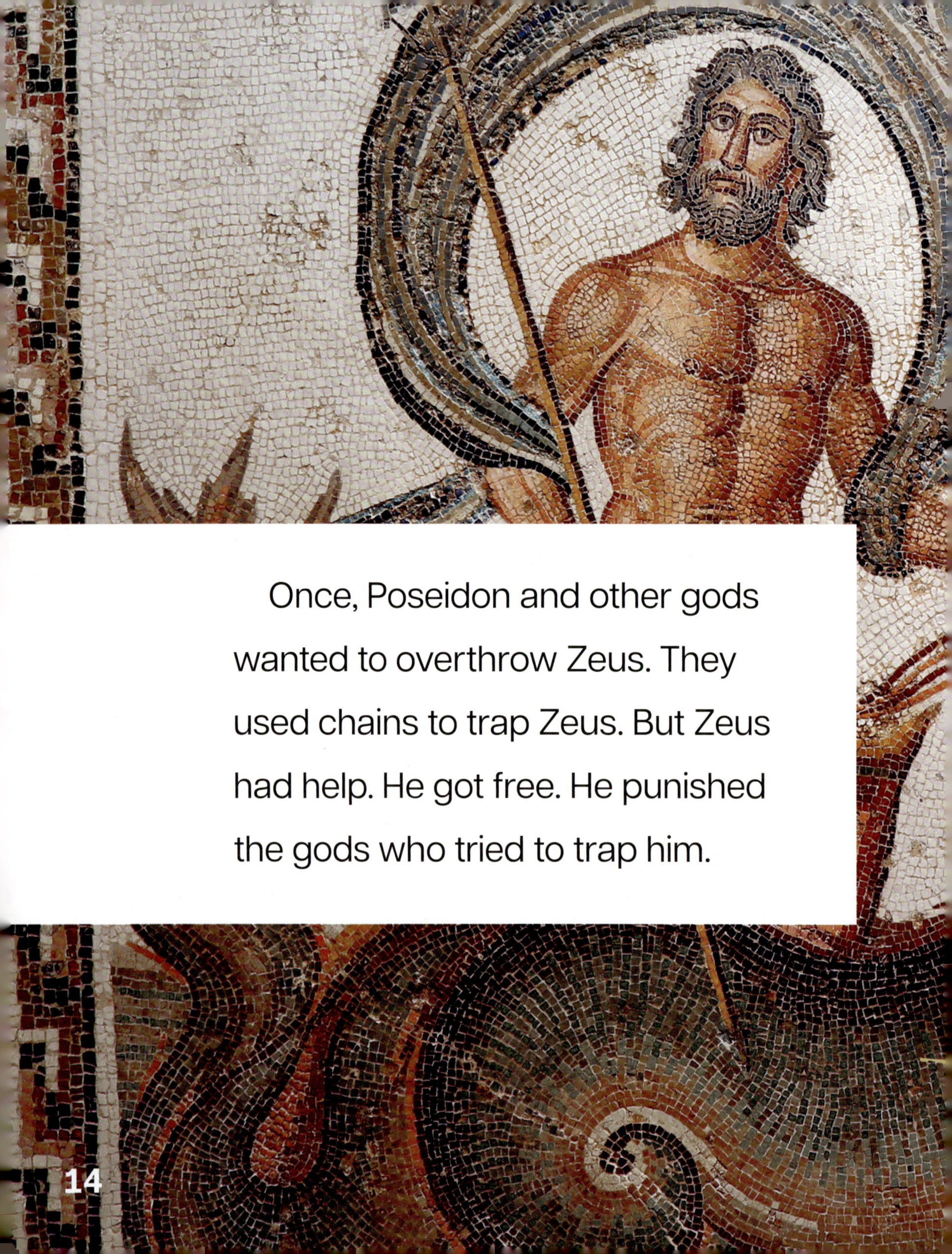

Once, Poseidon and other gods wanted to overthrow Zeus. They used chains to trap Zeus. But Zeus had help. He got free. He punished the gods who tried to trap him.

In art, hippocampi often have fins like fish. Some even have scales on parts of their bodies.

POSEIDON'S RIDE

Poseidon often rode in a **chariot**. Creatures called hippocampi pulled it. Each creature had the upper body of a horse. Its lower body looked like a fish.

CHAPTER 3

ACTS OF ANGER

Like the waters he ruled, Poseidon was unpredictable. He got angry easily. And he could be **vengeful**.

Poseidon caused lots of problems for people he didn't like.

Once, Poseidon helped build walls around a city. The city's king didn't want to pay him. So, Poseidon got very angry. He sent a sea monster to attack the city.

According to legend, Poseidon could yell as loud as ten thousand men combined.

Poseidon helped build walls for the city of Troy.

Cetus is a constellation in the night sky. This group of stars is named after a sea monster Poseidon sent to attack people.

The sea monster grabbed people who came near the shore. But a hero killed it.

ANOTHER ATTACK

In one story, a queen bragged that her daughter was prettier than all the sea nymphs. Poseidon got mad. He sent a sea monster to kill the daughter. A hero saved her.

CHAPTER 4

HONORING POSEIDON

Poseidon was popular throughout Greece. But he was especially important along the coasts. Many of his temples were near bodies of water.

Greece has almost 8,500 miles (13,700 km) of coastline.

Part of Poseidon's temple at Cape Sounion still stands today.

For example, one famous temple was built on **Cape** Sounion. Another stood on the **Isthmus** of Corinth. This area was part of a major trade route. From there, ships sailed around the world.

POSEIDON'S CITY

Poseidon was the **patron** of Corinth. Every two years, the city held a **festival** in his honor. It featured music and sports. There were horse races as well.

In Rome, Poseidon was known by the name Neptune.

At temples, people made **offerings** to Poseidon. They asked for safe travels. And they requested help with fishing and trade.

Sea bass was one type of fish that people caught in ancient Greece.

Some places held boat races to honor Poseidon.

TEST YOUR KNOWLEDGE

Take this quiz to test your knowledge.

1. Write a few sentences describing the main ideas of Chapter 2.

2. Would you rather have the power to cause earthquakes or to create storms? Why?

3. Which creatures pulled Poseidon's chariot?

   A. fish
   B. nymphs
   C. hippocampi

4. Why were Poseidon's temples built near water?

   A. Most of Poseidon's powers involved water.
   B. Poseidon disliked water and avoided it.
   C. Poseidon had no powers on land.

5. What does **unpredictable** mean in this book?

Like the waters he ruled, Poseidon was ***unpredictable****. He got angry easily.*

- **A.** never getting angry
- **B.** always staying calm
- **C.** often changing moods

6. What does **requested** mean in this book?

They asked for safe travels. And they ***requested*** *help with fishing and trade.*

- **A.** stood next to something
- **B.** asked for something
- **C.** fell off something

Answers can be found on page 32.

GLOSSARY

cape
A narrow area of land that sticks out into a body of water.

chariot
A two-wheeled cart pulled by horses or other animals.

festival
A day or time of celebration, often based on a religion.

isthmus
A thin strip of land that connects two large areas of land.

nymphs
Beautiful spirits that live in trees, water, or other parts of nature.

offerings
Gifts to a god or goddess to get his or her help or favor.

patron
A person who gives help or support.

trident
A spear with three points.

vengeful
Wanting to hurt someone who has hurt you.

FOR MORE INFORMATION

BOOKS

Hudak, Heather C. *Poseidon*. Minneapolis, MN: Abdo Publishing, 2022.

MacCarald, Clara. *Greek Mythology Monsters*. San Diego, CA: BrightPoint Press, 2022.

WEBSITES

Britannica Kids: Poseidon

kids.britannica.com/kids/article/Poseidon/353659

Read more about Poseidon.

National Geographic Kids: The Gods and Goddesses of Ancient Greece!

natgeokids.com/nz/discover/history/greece/greek-gods

Learn more about Greek gods and goddesses.

Publisher's note to educators and parents: Our editors have carefully reviewed these websites to ensure that they are suitable for students. Many websites change frequently, however, and we cannot guarantee that a site's future contents will continue to meet our high standards of quality and educational value. Be advised that students should be closely supervised whenever they access the internet.

INDEX

Answer Key:
1. Answers will vary; 2. Answers will vary; 3. C; 4. A; 5. C; 6. B